TEST PREP MATH BOOK
FOR CASAS MATH GOALS 2 LEVEL C

Helping Learners Approach Math with Confidence while Preparing them for CASAS Math GOALS 2 Level C—**Forms 925M and 926M**

By

TABLE OF CONTENT

PREFACE

Dear Instructors,

This Test Prep math book is specifically designed to prepare adult learners for the CASAS Math GOALS 2 Level C Forms 925M and 926M. It fully aligns with the CASAS Competencies and meets the requirements of the College and Career Reading Standards (CCRS), the National Reporting System (NRS), and the Workforce Innovation and Opportunity Act (WIOA).

Adhering to the CASAS test blueprint, this textbook covers mathematical areas through six detailed chapters: *Number Sense and Operations, Consumer Economics, Algebraic Thinking, Geometry, Data Analysis, Statistics and Probability, and Pure Mathematics.*

The book's content is structured to improve the mathematical thinking skills of adult students. It provides 13 lessons across various competencies, such as Consumer Economics, Community Resources, Employment, and Pure Mathematics. Each chapter is thoughtfully crafted with multiple lessons to foster deep understanding and practical application of mathematical concepts.

Additionally, the book includes a practice test that simulates the actual CASAS assessments, incorporating real-world math problems to give students a genuine taste of what they can expect. Complete with answer keys for all exercises and practice tests, this textbook is a robust tool for effective learning and assessment.

Using this resource in your teaching will equip you to effectively develop and improve the math strategies, functions, and concepts necessary for your adult learners' success. Indeed, this book is an invaluable asset for programs that aim to empower their students with the mathematical skills required for success in everyday contexts such as community involvement, family management, and professional environments. To order class sets, go to cbledu.com.

INTRODUCTION

Dear Math Students,

Welcome to your journey toward improving your math skills with this test-prep math textbook. It is designed specifically for adult learners like you. This book is structured to prepare you for the CASAS Math GOALS 2 Level C test. In the six chapters, you'll explore essential mathematical areas, including *Number Sense and Operations, Consumer Economics, Algebraic Thinking, Geometry, Data Analysis, Statistics and Probability, and Pure Mathematics.* With 13 practical lessons, this textbook offers a clear path to improving your mathematical knowledge.

Practicing the exercises in this book is crucial. Each chapter includes multiple lessons that build on each other to help you understand and apply mathematical concepts in real-world situations. By engaging with these exercises, you'll develop a stronger foundation in each topic, making sure that you're well-prepared not just for the tests but also for the practical application of these skills in daily life.

We've also included a practice test that mimics the actual CASAS level C test. This practice test is designed to give you a realistic experience of what to expect on the actual test. By taking it, you can assess your progress, identify areas where you need further practice, and build your confidence.

This textbook is more than just a study guide—it's a tool that will equip you with the math strategies, functions, and concepts necessary to solve word problems confidently. Regular practice and study will transform your understanding of math, turning challenges into opportunities for growth and learning.

Remember, math skills are essential for success in various aspects of your life, including community involvement, managing family finances, and professional advancement. By committing to completing the exercises and fully engaging with the materials in this book, you'll be setting yourself up for success in your academic pursuits and beyond.

Let's get started on this path together!

HOW TO APPROACH MATH

Here are ten practical ways you can overcome math fear and anxiety and build confidence while using this math textbook:

1. **Start Small:** Begin with easier problems that you can solve to build your confidence before solving harder ones.

2. **Practice Regularly:** Consistent practice makes math feel more manageable. Try to work on math problems a few times a week.

3. **Use the Book's Resources:** Take advantage of the tools and explanations in your textbook. They are designed to help you understand and solve math problems.

4. **Take Breaks:** If you feel overwhelmed, take a short break. Come back to the problem with a clear mind.

5. **Ask for Help:** Don't hesitate to seek help when you need it. Ask a teacher, a classmate, or use online resources if you're stuck.

6. **Stay Positive:** Keep a positive attitude about math. Remind yourself that you can handle it and that it's okay to make mistakes as you learn.

7. **Set Small Goals:** Break your math studies into small, achievable goals. Celebrate when you reach these goals to motivate yourself.

8. **Understand, Don't Memorize:** Focus on understanding the math concepts rather than just memorizing formulas. This understanding will make you feel more confident in your ability to solve math problems.

9. **Visualize Success:** Picture yourself successfully solving problems and understanding concepts. This visualization can boost your confidence.

10. **Reflect on Progress:** Regularly look back at where you started and recognize the progress you've made. This can be a great confidence booster.

By following these strategies, you'll be better positioned to tackle math with less anxiety and more confidence.

STUDY STRATEGIES

Here are ten simple strategies for studying and improving your math knowledge, skills, and understanding using this textbook. Each strategy is designed to be practical and straightforward.

Strategy	Description
1. Set a study schedule.	Allocate specific times each week for math study and practice to build a routine.
2. Create a study space.	Find a quiet, organized space dedicated to studying to stay focused.
3. Use the textbook.	Read explanations and solve problems in the textbook to understand concepts deeply.
4. Practice with examples.	Work through example problems to understand how to apply math rules before trying exercises on your own.
5. Summarize each lesson.	Write a brief summary of what you learned in each lesson to reinforce your understanding.
6. Solve practice tests.	Use practice tests in the textbook to prepare for the actual test and build confidence.
7. Discuss with peers.	Study in groups or discuss problems with classmates to get different perspectives and solutions.
8. Teach someone else.	Explain math concepts to someone else to improve your own understanding and retention.
9. Use online resources.	Supplement your textbook with online tutorials and exercises (e.g., YouTube videos) for additional practice.
10. 1Review regularly.	Regularly go back and review previous chapters to keep information fresh and build connections between topics and chapters.

Using these strategies can help you make the most of your math textbook and your study time to gradually build up your mathematical abilities and confidence.

Lesson 1: Perform the four operations with whole numbers, decimals and fractions.

We can solve problems using the four operations with whole numbers, decimals, and fractions. The operations are addition, subtraction, multiplication, and division.

Example 1:

A company took 162 employees to a management conference across the country. Each round-trip plane ticket cost $515.89. What was the total amount needed to take the employees to the conference?

Solution:

Notice that this is a multiplication problem. Then, multiply 515.89 by 162. Ignore the decimal points and multiply the numbers as whole numbers.

$$
\begin{array}{r}
51589 \ \times \\
162 \\
\hline
103178 \ + \\
309534 \\
51589 \\
\hline
8357418
\end{array}
$$

Now, we must place the decimal point. Notice that 515.89 has **two** decimal digits. Then, the product will have **two** decimal digits.

$$83{,}574.18$$

So the total amount needed to take the employees to the conference is **$83,574.18**

Example 2:

An elephant will eat about 2,583 pounds of vegetation in 3 weeks. What is the average amount an elephant will eat in a day?

Solution:

First, we convert 3 weeks to days.

3 weeks = 3 x 7 days = 21 days

We know that the average is equal to the number of pounds divided by the number of days, so we divide 2,583 by 21.

$$
\begin{array}{r}
123 \\
2583 \,\big|\, 21 \\
\underline{21} \\
48 \\
\underline{42} \\
63 \\
\underline{63} \\
0
\end{array}
$$

Thus, the elephant will eat **123 pounds per day.**

Example 3:

Mrs. Parks needs to order pizza for 20 students. Each student should get ¼ of a pizza.

How many pizzas should Mrs. Parks order?

Solution:

To find the number of pizzas, we must multiply the number of students by the fraction of the pizza each student gets.

Step 1: Rewrite the whole number as a fraction. To rewrite a whole number as a fraction, simply place the whole number over 1.

$$
\frac{20}{1}
$$

Step 2: Multiply the fractions.

$$\frac{20}{1} \times \frac{1}{4} = \frac{20}{4}$$

Step 3: Simplify the fractions.

$$= \frac{20}{4} = 5$$

Then, Mrs. Parks should order **5 pizzas.**

Practice Exercises

1. What is the result of 2,054 x 4.5?

    A. 924.3

    B. 92.43

    C. 9200.43

    D. 9243

> Derrick makes $28.50 per hour.
>
> He worked 32 hours in one week.

2. How much money will Derrick earn in six weeks if he works 32 hours per week?

    A. $5,187

    B. $5,472

    C. $2,736

    D. $4,512

3. How much money will Derrick earn in one week?

    A. $900

    B. $889

    C. $912

    D. 915

4. If Derrick wants to purchase a motorcycle that costs $12,650, how many weeks does he have to work?

   A. 14

   B. 13

   C. 10

   D. 12

5. Which of the following is true?

   A. 1.5 x 2,000 = 300

   B. 1,000,000 + 50,000 = 1,500,000

   C. ¼ + 0.75 = 1

   D. 15,000 ÷ 5,000 = 30

6. Alex purchased a car for $10,980 and spent $3,235 on repairs. How much did the car cost him?

   A. $7,745

   B. $13,215

   C. $8,765

   D. $14,215

7. Briana gets $12.65 a week for chores and helps with chores for eight weeks. If she wants to spend only half of her money, how much will she have left to save?

   A. $50.60

   B. $100.20

   C. $60.50

   D. $50.20

8. Judy bought a smart TV for $249.99 and a tablet for $179.99. The sales tax was $22.50. How much did Judy spend?

   A. $452.48

   B. $429.28

   C. $272.49

   D. $467.89

9. A large tank truck can hold up to 12,400 gallons of water. If the truck already contains ¾ of the capacity of the tank truck, how many more gallons will be required to fill the tanker?

   A. 9,300 gal

   B. 3,100 gal.

   C. 3,200 gal.

   D. 3,150 gal.

10. Compute

$$(1,456 + 986) \div (167 - 161)$$

   A. 146

   B. 306

   C. 412

   D. 407

Answer Key:

1) D

2) B

3) C

4) A

5) C

6) D

7) A

8) A

9) B

10) D

Lesson 2: Understand ratio, rate and percent concepts.

A **ratio** is a way to show a relationship or compare two numbers of the same kind. We can write ratios in different ways, and they all mean the same thing.

Here are some of the ways we can write ratios:

2 is to 5

2:5

2/5

A **rate** is a ratio of two quantities having different units. A **unit rate** is a rate where the second quantity is one unit, such as $15 per gallon or 45 miles per hour. "Per gallon" and "per hour" are the second quantities in each ratio.

Percent means "out of 100." We can use the percent symbol (%) as a way to write a fraction with a common denominator of 100. For example, instead of saying, "28 out of the 100 animals are ducks," we can say, "28% of the animals are ducks."

In other words,

20% means $\dfrac{20}{100} = \dfrac{1}{5}$

A percent can also be expressed as a **fraction**. To convert a fraction to a percent, we divide the top number (numerator) by the bottom number (denominator). We then multiply the result by 100 and add the "%" sign.

Example 1:

A copy machine makes 120 copies in 40 seconds. Find the unit rate of copies per second.

Solution:

Divide 120 by 40 to find the unit rate.

$$\frac{120}{40} = 3$$

Then, the copy machine makes **3 copies per second.**

Example 2:

Convert 2/5 to a percent.

Solution:

Step 1: Divide 2 by 5:

$2 \div 5 = 0.4$

Step 2: Multiply the result by 100 and add the "%" sign:

0.4 x 100% = 40%

Thus, 2/ 5 = **40%**

Example 3:

An item originally costs $260. If the price of the item increases by 15%, what is the new price?

Solution:

Step 1: First, convert 15% to a fraction.

$$15\% = \frac{15}{100}$$

Step 2: Simplify the fraction.

$$\frac{15}{100} = \frac{3}{20}$$

Step 3: Multiply $\frac{3}{20}$ by 260.

$$\frac{3}{20} \times 260 = \frac{780}{20} = 39$$

Step 4: The item's price has increased by $39. Thus, we add $39 and $260.

$260 + $39= **$299**

So, the new price is $299.

Practice Exercises

1. Which of the following is a ratio?

   A. 45%

   B. 20 people/3 hours

   C. 0.26

   D. 3/7

2. Which of the following is a rate?

   A. 3 miles

   B. 8 pounds / 2 dollars

   C. 5 : 6

   D. 3.5%

> In a classroom with 24 students, there are six students with blue shoes, 10 with black shoes, and 8 with white shoes.

3. What is the ratio of students with blue shoes to those with black shoes?

   A. 5/3

   B. 2/5

   C. 3/5

   D. 3/10

4. What is the ratio of students with black shoes to those with white shoes?

   A. 5/4

   B. 4/5

   C. 5/6

   D. 4/3

5. What is the ratio of students with white shoes to all the students in the class?

   A. 24/8

   B. 4/8

   C. 8/5

   D. 1/3

6. Which of the following is a unit rate?

   A. 7:8

   B. 45 feet per second

   C. $8/ 3 weeks

   D. 100%

7. A baseball pitcher won 40% of the games he pitched. If he pitched 15 games, how many games did he win?

   A. 8

   B. 10

   C. 6

   D. 7

8. Eddie scored 60 out of 80 in a math test. What percent was that?

   A. 60%

   B. 70%

   C. 80%

   D. 75%

9. Ms. Wallace bought a car for $22,500. After 6 years, its value depreciated by 10%. What is the value of the car after 6 years?

   A. $24,750

   B. $20,250

   C. $21,750

   D. $20,500

10. Which of the following is true?

   A. 2/9 is a unit rate.

   B. 1% = 1/10

   C. 100% of 57 is 57.

   D. 50% of 40 is 30.

Answer Key:

1) D

2) B

3) C

4) A

5) D

6) B

7) C

8) D

9) B

10) C

Lesson 3: The Properties of Integer Exponents

The **exponent** of a number says **how many times** to use the number in a multiplication.

$$\text{Base} \implies 2^3 = 2 \times 2 \times 2 = 8$$

Exponents are also called **Powers** or **Indices**.

Properties of Integer Exponents

<u>Multiplication of powers with the same base</u>: When we multiply powers with the same base, we must **add** the exponents and keep the base.

$$a^m \cdot a^n = a^{m+n}$$

<u>Division of powers with the same base</u>: When we divide powers with the same base, we have to **subtract** the exponents and keep the base.

$$\frac{a^m}{a^n} = a^{m-n}$$

<u>Powers to powers</u>: To raise a power to a power, we must **multiply** the exponents and keep the base.

$$(a^m)^n = a^{m \cdot n}$$

<u>Negative exponent</u>: A number with a negative exponent is the reciprocal of that number with a positive exponent.

$$a^{-n} = \frac{1}{a^n}$$

<u>Zero exponent</u>: Any nonzero number raised to the power of 0 is equal to 1.

$$a^0 = 1$$

Example 1:

Simplify the following expression:

$$\frac{2^5 \cdot 2^3}{2^6}$$

Solution:

Step 1: First, apply the multiplication of powers with the same base property in the numerator:

$$2^5 \cdot 2^3 = 2^{5+3} = 2^8$$

Then, we get

$$\frac{2^8}{2^6}$$

Step 2: Apply the division of powers with the same base property.

$$\frac{2^8}{2^6} = 2^{8-6} = 2^2$$

Step 3: Simplify.

$$2^2 = 2 \times 2 = 4$$

Thus, the result is:

$$\frac{2^5 \cdot 2^3}{2^6} = 4$$

Example 2:

Simplify

$$\left(\frac{5^{10}}{5^4}\right)^{-2}$$

Solution:

Step 1: First, apply the division of powers with the same base property:

$$\frac{5^{10}}{5^4} = 5^{10-4} = 5^6$$

Then, we get:

$$(5^6)^{-2}$$

Step 2: Apply the negative exponent property:

$$(5^6)^{-2} = \frac{1}{(5^6)^2}$$

Step 3: Apply the power to power property:

$$\frac{1}{(5^6)^2} = \frac{1}{5^{6 \cdot 2}} = \frac{1}{5^{12}}$$

Then, we get:

$$\left(\frac{5^{10}}{5^4}\right)^{-2} = \frac{1}{5^{12}}$$

Practice Exercises

1. Simplify the following expression

$$\frac{10^{20}}{10^{15}}$$

   A. 10^{35}

   B. 10^{300}

   C. 10^5

   D. 10

2. Which of the following is equivalent to the following expression?

$$\frac{3^8 \cdot 3^6 \cdot 3^6}{3^{18}}$$

   A. 3^{38}

   B. 3^{12}

   C. 3^3

   D. 9

3. Which of the following is true?

   A. $(7^7)^7 = 7^{49}$

   B. $(12)^0 = 0$

   C. $3^{12} + 3^{12} = 3^{24}$

   D. $4^4 = 16$

4. What is the value of m?

$$x^9 \cdot x^m = x^{16}$$

   A. 25

   B. 7

   C. 6

   D. 8

5. The distance between the Earth and a star is 2^{70} light-years. What is half of this distance?

   A. 2^{35} light-years

   B. 1^{70} light-years

   C. 1^{35} light-years

   D. 2^{69} light-years

6. Which expression is equivalent to $\frac{1}{16}$?

   A. 4^2

   B. 2^4

   C. 4^{-2}

   D. 16^0

7. What is the value of p?

$$(8^8)^p = 8^{40}$$

   A. 32

   B. 6

   C. 5

   D. 4

8. An enormous rock weighs 10^5 kilograms. The weight of a meteorite is ten times the weight of the rock. What is the weight of the meteorite?

   A. 20^5 kg

   B. 10^{50} kg

C. 100^5 kg

D. 10^6 kg

9. Simply the following expression:

$$\frac{b^5 \cdot b^{12} \cdot b^8}{b^7 \cdot b^{18}}$$

A. 1

B. b

C. b^2

D. 0

10. Which of the following is equivalent to 4^{13}?

A. 2^{14}

B. 2^{26}

C. 2^{52}

D. 2^{13}

Answer Key:

1) C

2) D

3) A

4) B

5) D

6) C

7) C

8) D

9) A

10) B

Answer the following reflection questions and feel free to discuss your responses with your teacher or a classmate.

1- What math ideas and principles did you learn in this chapter?

2- What new math concepts did you learn?

3- What procedures or methods did you practice in this chapter?

4- What aspect of this chapter is still not 100% clear to you?

5- What else do you want your teacher to know?

CHAPTER 2:
CONSUMER ECONOMICS

Lesson 1: Use measurement and money.

People use money every day, and being able to count it and work out how much change they should be left with is an important life skill. The currency of the US is the United States Dollar (USD). Its symbol is $. American bills or paper currency comes in seven denominations: $1, $2, $5, $10, $20, $50, and $100.

The most commonly used coins in US money are quarters, dimes, nickels, and pennies.

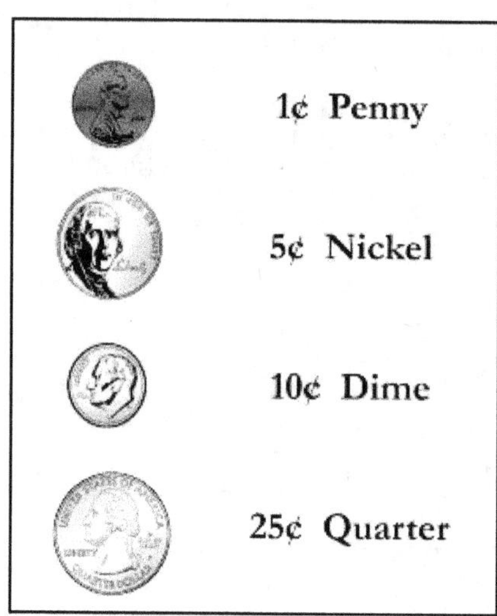

Converting Dollars and Cents

1 dollar = 100 cents, so 1 cent is equal to 0.01 dollars.

1 nickel = 5 cents, so 1 nickel is equal to 0.05 dollars.

1 dime = 10 cents, so 1 dime is equal to 0.1 dollars.

1 quarter = 25 cents, so 1 quarter is equal to 0.25 dollars.

Example 1:

A packet of candy costs 89 cents, and a bottle of milk costs $14.50. Melinda buys five packets of candy and two bottles of milk. She pays with a 50-dollar bill. How much change does she get?

Solution:

Step 1: First, convert 89 cents to a dollar:

89 cents = 0.89 dollars

Step 2: Calculate the cost of five packets of candy.

5 x $0.89 = $4.45

Step 3: Calculate the cost of two bottles of milk.

2 x $14.50 = $29

Step 4: Add up the total cost.

$4.45 +$29 = $33.45

Step 5: To calculate the change, subtract $33.45 from $50.

$50 – $33.45 = $16.55

Thus, Melinda gets **$16.55** in change.

Measurement is a system used to determine the length, weight, capacity, time or number of certain objects. Here is a list of units of measurement we use to measure various objects:

Length or Height (centimeters, meters, kilometers, feet, miles)

Weight (milligrams, grams, kilograms, ounces, pounds, tons)

Volume (milliliters, liters, quarts, gallons)

Time (seconds, hours, weeks, months, years)

Money (dollars, euros, pesos, yen)

Temperature (Celsius degrees, Fahrenheit degrees)

Example 2:

How many kilometers are there in 4,500 meters?

Solution:

We know that 1 kilometer = 1,000 meters. To convert smaller units (meters) to larger units (kilometers), we **divide** the number of smaller units by 1,000.

4,500 m = 4,500 ÷ 1,000 = **4.5 km**

Practice Exercises

> Rick buys three pens at 69 cents each, four folders at $1.29 each, and a pencil case at $1.89.

1. What is the total cost?

    A. $7.23

    B. $9.12

    C. $8.89

    D. $9.23

2. If Rick pays with a 10-dollar bill, how much change does he get?

    A. $0.18

    B. 88 cents

    C. $0.90

    D. 8 cents

3. What is the cost of a dozen pens?

    A. 82 cents

    B. $4.14

    C. $8.28

    D. 830 cents

4. What is the cost of ten pencil cases?

    A. $19.80

    B. $20.90

    C. $17.99

    D. $18.90

5. Which of the following is the correct measuring unit for the weight of a banana?

    A. Pounds

    B. Gallons

    C. Tons

    D. Yards

6. Which of the following is the correct unit to measure the height of a giraffe?

    A. Inches

    B. Centimeters

    C. Liters

    D. Feet

7. Latrell has three 10-dollar bills, 10 quarters, and 20 dimes. How much money does he have?

    A. $34.50

    B. $32.50

    C. $30.45

    D. $32.00

8. Which of the following is true?

    A. 1,000 pennies = $10

    B. $150 = 500 quarters

    C. 100 meters = 1 kilometer

    D. 1 mile is less than 5,000 feet

9. A baby elephant weighs 330 pounds. The weight of its mom is 16 times as much. What is the weight of its mom in tons? (Hint: 1 ton = 2,000 pounds)

   A. 2.20 tons

   B. 2.64 tons

   C. 3.50 tons

   D. 1.32 tons

10. Roger claims there are X quarters in $500. What is X?

   A. 1,000

   B. 2,500

   C. 2,000

   D. 1,500

Answer Key:

1) B

2) B

3) C

4) D

5) A

6) D

7) A

8) A

9) B

10) C

Lesson 2: Use information to identify and purchase goods and services.

A good is a physical item that can be bought, touched, and used. A service is an action done for people who pay for it.

To obtain the best deal, we compare the cost of two or more items and then decide which has the best value.

To compare prices, divide the cost by the weight or quantity of the item. Then, we can compare the two items. In other words, to compare prices, we compare the **unit rates** of the items.

Example 1:

At Super Market 2000, Brittany could get 5 pants for $125. At an online shop, the price for 8 pants is $184. Which is the best deal?

Solution:

Find the unit price for each place:

Super Market 2000:

$$unit\ rate = \frac{\$125}{5} = \$25\ per\ pants$$

Online Store:

$$unit\ rate = \frac{\$184}{8} = \$23\ per\ pants$$

Then, the best deal is 8 pants for $184 **(lower unit rate)**

Reading bills and receipts is a life skill because almost every household receives at least one type of bill or receipt each month. Understanding how to read bills and receipts can help us budget our money.

Example 2:

According to the following receipt, what is the total cost?

<table>
<tr><td colspan="3" align="center">Food Business Center
23232, JAVA CITY, SELANGOR
NY, USA
TEL : 03-435435435</td></tr>
<tr><td colspan="3"><h2>Table - 06</h2></td></tr>
<tr><td>Check #:
Date :
Cashier:</td><td>622967
11/01/2020
David Smith</td><td>Pax(s): 04
18:34</td></tr>
<tr><td>4</td><td>Chinese Buffet</td><td align="right">51.96</td></tr>
<tr><td>4</td><td>Soda</td><td align="right">7.96</td></tr>
<tr><td>4</td><td>Desserts</td><td align="right">15.56</td></tr>
<tr><td colspan="2">Subtotal :</td><td align="right">75.48</td></tr>
<tr><td colspan="2">Food Tax</td><td align="right">2.90</td></tr>
<tr><td colspan="2">Local Tax</td><td align="right">1.28</td></tr>
<tr><td colspan="2"><h2>Total :</h2></td><td align="right"><h2>?</h2></td></tr>
</table>

Solution:

To find the total amount, add subtotal, food tax and local tax:

Total amount = $75.48 + $2.90 + $1.28 = **$79.66**

Practice Exercises

Look at the following receipt:

```
              LOWE'S HOME CENTER, LLC
              1101 BEAVER CREEK COMMONS
                  APEX, NC, 34343
                   (888) 232 2323

                     - SALE -
   SALES#: S86614388236618 TRANS#: 11219309 05/11/2021

        1-CU FT COMPOSTED BLACK K              21.12
            2 @ 10.56
        2-CU FT COMPOSTED WHITE K              69.69
            3 @ 23.23
        SOLID BRICKS                           23.80
            20 @ 1.19
        ROSE PLANTS                            89.00
            10 @ 8.90

                    SUBTOTAL :               203.61
               SALES TAX 7.8% :               10.23
        INVOICE 19305 TOTAL :                    ?
                        VISA :

   VISA: XXXXXXXXXXXX AMOUNT:213.84 AUTHCD:J7AEOS
   CHIP REFID:927639501767 05/11/2021 22:31:57
         APL:CHASE VISA TVR:186974119814
         AID:3470942513772519 TSI:HU9A
```

1. How many items were purchased?

    A. 4

    B. 25

    C. 35

    D. 12

2. Which item is the cheapest?

    A. Rose plants

    B. Solid bricks

    C. 1-cu ft. composted black k

    D. 2-cu ft. composted white k

3. Which item is the most expensive?

   A. 1-cu ft. composted black k

   B. Solid bricks

   C. Rose plants

   D. 2-cu ft. composted white k

4. What is the total amount?

   A. $213.84

   B. $203.61

   C. $223.85

   D. $212.56

5. What is the cost of 30 rose plants?

   A. $119

   B. $250

   C. $267

   D. $297

Look at the following table:

Gas Station	Number of gallons	Cost
1	30	$114
2	25	$91.25
3	40	$119.60

6. What is the unit price for Gas Station 1 in dollars per gallon?

   A. $2.95 per gallon

   B. $3.80 per gallon

   C. $3.50 per gallon

   D. $2.78 per gallon

7. What is the best deal?

    A. Gas Station 3

    B. Gas Station 1

    C. Gas Station 2

8. What is the cost of 50 gallons of gas at Gas Station 2?

    A. $150

    B. $180.65

    C. $182.50

    D. $190

9. If Bob has $50 to spend on gas, what is the maximum number of gallons he can buy at Gas Station 1?

    A. 15 gallons

    B. 13 gallons

    C. 10 gallons

    D. 20 gallons

10. What is the best deal?

    A. 10 liters for $4

    B. 60 liters for $12

    C. 2 liters for $0.8

    D. 50 liters for $25

1) C

2) B

3) D

4) A

5) C

6) B

7) A

8) C

9) B

10) B

Answer the following reflection questions and feel free to discuss your responses with your teacher or a classmate.

1- What math ideas and principles did you learn in this chapter?

2- What new math concepts did you learn?

3- What procedures or methods did you practice in this chapter?

4- What aspect of this chapter is still not 100% clear to you?

5- What else do you want your teacher to know?

CHAPTER 3: ALGEBRAIC THINKING

Lesson 1: Solve simple one-variable equations and simple inequalities.

An **equation** is a mathematical statement that two things or expressions are equal. In an equation, the left side is always equal to the right side. The most common equations contain one or more **variables**. A **variable** is a symbol for a number we don't know yet. It is usually a letter like x or y, but we can use any letter.

Simple one-variable equation:

$$4x + 8 = 12$$

Solving a simple one-variable equation means **finding the value of the variable that makes the two expressions equal.** To solve an equation, follow these steps:

1. Figure out what to remove to get the value of the variable.

2. To remove a number, add its opposite to both sides.

We can solve word problems using equations with letters representing the **unknown numbers** in simple contextual math situations or real-life and mathematical problems.

Example 1:

Solve the equation $5x - 6 = 24$

Solution:

We want to remove 6 from the equation. To remove 6, do the opposite. In this case, add 6 to both sides of the equation.

$5x - 6 + 6 = 24 + 6$

$5x = 30$

We want to remove 5 from the equation. To remove 5, do the opposite. In this case, divide both sides of the equation by 5.

$$\frac{5x}{5} = \frac{30}{5}$$

x = 6

Example 2:

The cost of a jacket and a book is \$144. If the book costs \$28 less than the jacket, find the cost of the jacket and the book.

Solution:

Step 1: Let x be the cost of the jacket. Then, the cost of the book is x – 28.

Step 2: Set up the equation that represents the problem:

x + (x – 28) = 144

Step 3: Solve the equation. Combine like terms:

x + x – 28 = 144

2x – 28 = 144

Step 4: We want to remove 28 from the equation. To remove 28, do the opposite. In this case, add 28 to both sides of the equation.

2x – 28 + 28 = 144 + 28

2x = 172

Step 5: We want to remove 2 in the equation. To remove 2, do the opposite. In this case, divide both sides of the equation by 2.

$$\frac{2x}{2} = \frac{172}{2}$$

x = **86**

Thus, the cost of the jacket is **\$86,** and the cost of the book is \$86 – \$28 = **\$58**.

Inequalities are expressions in which two values are compared using the inequality symbols. Solving an inequality means finding a set of values that make the inequality true.

> **Inequality**
>
> $8x + 15 \leq 9$

The symbols which represent inequalities are:

> < (less than)
>
> \> (greater than)
>
> ≤ (less than or equal to)
>
> ≥ (greater than or equal to)

To solve a linear inequality, we follow the same steps as solving simple one-variable equations. Usually, we begin by isolating the variable from the numbers. However, it is important to remember to reverse the inequality sign when multiplying or dividing by negative numbers.

We can use inequalities to solve real-world problems. Some of the key words and phrases that indicate inequalities are summarized below:

> *At least* → means greater than or equal to (≥)
>
> *No more than* → means less than or equal to (≤)
>
> *More than* → means greater than (>)
>
> *Less than* → means less than (<)

Example 3:

Mike has $3,000 in a savings account. He wants to have at least $625 in the account by the end of the year. He withdraws $95 each week for food and entertainment. How many weeks can Mike withdraw money from his account?

Solution:

Step 1: First, choose a variable for the number of weeks. Let x be the number of weeks. Mike wants the amount in his account to be at least $625 which means $625 or greater. So, we must use the symbol ≥.

Step 2: Set up the inequality that represents the problem.

$$3000 - 95x \geq 625$$

Step 3: Solve the inequality. Subtract 3000 from both sides.

$$3000 - 3000 - 95x \geq 625 - 3000$$

$$-95x \geq -2375$$

Step 4: Multiply both sides by -1 and reverse the inequality sign.

$$-1(-95x) \geq -1(2375)$$

$$95x \leq 2375$$

Step 5: Divide both sides by 95.

$$\frac{95x}{95} \leq \frac{2375}{95}$$

$$x \leq 25$$

Then, Mike can withdraw money from his account for up to **25 weeks.**

Practice Exercises

1. Solve the following equation.

$$7x - 8 = 41$$

    A. $x = 7$

    B. $x = 6$

    C. $x = -7$

    D. $x = 5$

2. Solve the following inequality.

$$3x + 8 < 35$$

    A. $x = 9$

    B. $x < 8$

    C. $x > 9$

    D. $x < 9$

3. Which equation represents this problem?

    A. $3n - n = 72$

    B. $n + 3 = 72$

    C. $3n + n = 72$

    D. $n + n + 3 = 72$

4. How many prescriptions did he have for decongestants?

    A. 24

    B. 16

    C. 21

    D. 18

5. How many prescriptions did he have for antibiotics?

    A. 21

    B. 36

    C. 28

    D. 54

6. What is the inequality that represents this problem?

    A. $10 + 0.80x \leq 50$

    B. $0.80 + 10x \geq 50$

C. $10 + 0.80x \geq 50$

D. $10 - 0.80x \geq 50$

7. How many people must she register to earn at least $50 for the day?

   A. 45

   B. 50

   C. 49

   D. 37

8. Solve the following inequality:

$$12 - y > 30$$

   A. $y < -18$

   B. $y > 18$

   C. $y < 18$

   D. $y = -18$

9. Solve the following equation:

$$100x = 10$$

   A. 10

   B. 100

   C. 0.1

   D. 0.1

10. When a number is added to itself twice, the answer is 84. What is the number?

   A. 42

   B. 28

   C. 32

   D. 41

1) A

2) D

3) C

4) D

5) D

6) C

7) B

8) C

9) C

10) B

Lesson 2: Understand relationships between dependent and independent variables.

An independent variable is a quantity that you can change in an equation. The letter **x** is often used to represent the independent variable.

A dependent variable is a quantity whose value depends on how the independent variable is changed. The letter **y** is often used to represent the dependent variable.

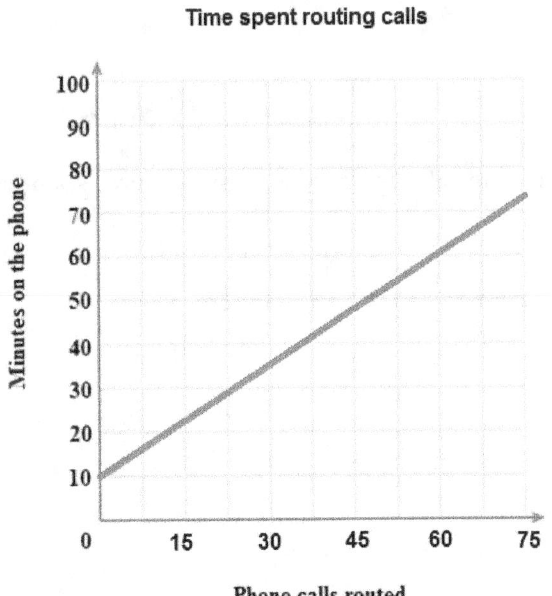

When we graph an equation, we usually put the independent variable on the **x**-axis (the horizontal line) and the dependent variable on the **y**-axis **(the vertical line)**. A graph helps us see how the independent and dependent variables are related.

Example 1:

The following graph shows how the amount of time a receptionist spends on the phone is related to the number of phone calls she routes to employees. If the receptionist routes 60 phone calls, how much time will she have spent on the phone in total?

Solution:

Step 1: We find 60 phone calls on the x-axis. Notice that the number of phone calls routed is the independent variable, and the number of minutes on the phone is the dependent variable.

Step 2: From 60 on the x-axis, we move up until we meet the graph line.

Step 3: We then move left to see the total time on the y-axis.

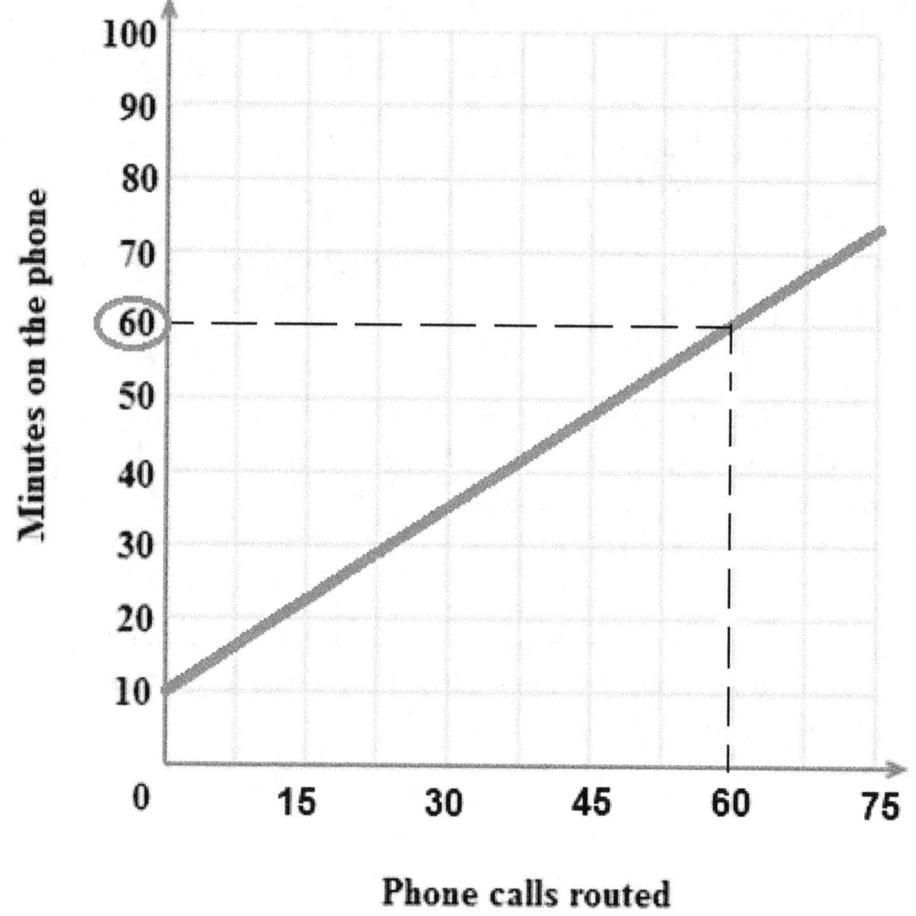

The graph shows that at 60 phone calls, the receptionist will have spent a total of **60 minutes** on the phone.

Practice Exercises

1. If h = 5t + 7 is an equation, then h is

    A. A dependent variable.

    B. An independent variable.

    C. A constant.

    D. A number.

> The total cost of gallons of milk purchased is represented by the following equation: C = 3.95n, where C is the total cost in dollars and n is the number of gallons of milk purchased.

2. What is the dependent variable?

    A. The number of gallons of milk purchased

    B. The unit price of milk

    C. 3.95 gallons of milk

    D. The total cost

3. What is the total cost of 20 gallons of milk?

    A. $23.85

    B. $78.50

    C. $79.00

    D. $77.95

4. If the total cost is $150.15, how many gallons of milk were purchased?

    A. 38

    B. 41

    C. 39

    D. 43

Study the following graph:

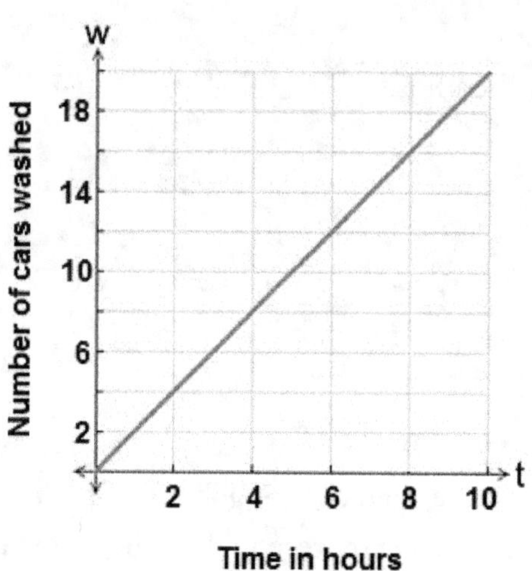

5. What is the independent variable?

    A. The number of cars washed

    B. The time in hours

    C. The unit rate in cars per hour

    D. Ten cars

6. How many cars were washed in six hours?

    A. 10

    B. 12

    C. 13

    D. 11

7. How long did it take to wash 16 cars?

    A. 9 hours

    B. 7 hours

    C. 8 hours

    D. 10 hours

8. If $T = 4.5m - 8$ is an equation, what is the independent variable?

    A. 8

    B. T

C. 4.5

D. m

9. Kathy spends 3 hours studying for a math test. What is the dependent variable in this situation?

A. The score on the math test

B. The number of hours spent studying

C. The number of questions on the math test

D. Cannot be determined

10. A music website charges \$28 per month plus \$3.50 as an additional fee for each song downloaded. What is the dependent variable in this situation?

A. The number of songs downloaded per month

B. The additional fee

C. The total cost per month

D. The cost of songs downloaded per month

Answer Key:

1) A

2) D

3) C

4) A

5) B

6) B

7) C

8) D

9) A

10) C

Lesson 3: Understand proportional relationships and linear equations.

When two values maintain **the same ratio**, forming the same fraction when we divide them, they have a **proportional relationship.**

This relationship can be represented by a linear equation of the form **y = mx**, where *m* is a constant. The constant, *m*, is called **the constant of proportionality**, the unit rate, or the slope.

A **linear equation** is an equation in which the highest power of the variable is always 1. The graph of a linear equation always forms a **straight line.**

To determine if a proportional relationship exists, check if the data points lie on a straight line that passes through the origin.

> **Proportional Relationship**
>
> $y = 4x$

Example 1:

The following table shows the time it takes to ride the elevator to three different floors of a building.

Floor number	3	6	9
Time needed (in seconds)	5	10	15

According to the table, is the floor number proportional to the time it takes to get there?

Solution:

Find the ratio to get to each floor. Write the ratio of Floor 3 as a fraction.

$$\frac{3}{5}$$

Write the ratio of Floor 6 as a fraction.

$$\frac{6}{10} = \frac{3}{5} \ (simplest \ form)$$

Write the ratio of Floor 9 as a fraction.

$$\frac{9}{15} = \frac{3}{5} \quad (simplest\ form)$$

Notice that we get **the same ratio** (equivalent fractions). Then, **the floor number is proportional to the time.**

We can also find the linear equation that represents this proportional relationship. Notice that the independent variable (x variable) is the time in seconds, and the dependent variable (y variable) is the floor number. The ratio $\frac{3}{5}$ is the constant of proportionality. Therefore, the linear equation that represents this proportional relationship is:

$$y = \frac{3}{5}x$$

Practice Exercises

1. Which of the following is a linear equation?

    A. $y = 3x^2$

    B. $h = 0.45$

    C. $s = 1.25t$

    D. $x = y^3$

The following table shows Kenny's earnings based on the number of hours he worked.

Number of Hours	2	4	6
Kenny's Earnings	$51	$102	$153

2. Are Kenny's earnings proportional to the number of hours he works?

    A. No

    B. Yes

    C. Cannot be determined

3. How much money does Kenny earn in eight hours?

   A. $200

   B. $208

   C. $204

   D. $212

4. What is the independent variable in this relationship?

   A. The number of hours

   B. Kenny's earnings

   C. The unit rate in dollars per hour

   D. The number of days

5. If x is the independent variable and y is the dependent variable, what is the linear equation representing this situation?

   A. $y = 15x$

   B. $y = 25.5x$

   C. $y = 25x$

   D. None of the above

6. What is Kenny's hourly wage?

   A. $20 per hour

   B. $25 per hour

   C. $26.25 per hour

   D. $25.50 per hour

> Amanda bought 12 hair spray bottles for $119.40. Let x be the
> number of hair spray bottles and y be the total cost of the hair spray.

7. What equation represents the proportional relationship between the total cost of the hair spray
   and the number of bottles purchased?

   A. $y = 9.95x$

   B. $x = 9.95y$

   C. $y = 0.10x$

   D. $y = 10x$

8. What is the cost of one hair spray bottle?

   A. $10.00

   B. $9.50

   C. $9.95

   D. $9.99

9. What is the cost of eight hair spray bottles?

   A. $79.20

   B. $79.60

   C. $80.00

   D. $72.50

10. Suppose that Amanda spends $298.50. How many hair spray bottles did she buy?

    A. 25

    B. 28

    C. 32

    D. 30

1) C

2) B

3) C

4) A

5) B

6) D

7) A

8) C

9) B

10) D

Answer the following reflection questions and feel free to discuss your responses with your teacher or a classmate.

1- What math ideas and principles did you learn in this chapter?

2- What new math concepts did you learn?

3- What procedures or methods did you practice in this chapter?

4- What aspect of this chapter is still not 100% clear to you?

5- What else do you want your teacher to know?

CHAPTER 4:
GEOMETRY

Lesson 1: Solve problems involving perimeter, area, surface area, and volume.

Here are some common terms to understand in geometry:

- **Perimeter** is the distance around a two-dimensional shape.

- **Area** is the amount of space inside a closed two-dimensional figure. A square with a side length of 1 unit, called a **unit square**, is said to have "one square unit" of area and can be used to measure area.

- A **square inch** is a unit of area equal to the area of a square with sides of one inch.

- The **surface area** of a three-dimensional object is the total area of all its faces.

- The **volume** is the amount of space occupied by a three-dimensional shape.

The Perimeter and Area of Common Two-Dimensional Shapes

		Perimeter	Area
Rectangle	Length (l), Width (w)	$P = 2(l + w)$	$A = l \times w$
Square	Length (x), Width (x)	$P = 4x$	$A = x^2$
Parallelogram	a, h, b	$P = 2(a + b)$	$A = a \times h$
Trapezoid	a, c, h, d, b	$P = a + b + c + d$	$A = \dfrac{(a + b) \times h}{2}$
Triangle	c, h, a, b	$P = a + b + c$	$A = \dfrac{b \times h}{2}$
Circle	r	$P = Circumference = 2\pi r \text{ or } \pi D$	$A = \pi \times r^2$

The Surface Area and Volume of Common Three-Dimensional Shapes

CUBE	CUBOID	CYLINDER
SURFACE AREA	**SURFACE AREA**	**SURFACE AREA**
TOTAL $A = 6l^2$	TOTAL $A = 2(ab + bc + ac)$	TOTAL $A = 2\pi r(r + h)$
SIDES $A = 4l^2$	SIDES $A = 2(ab + 2ac)$	CURVED $A = 2\pi rh$
VOLUME $V = l^3$	VOLUME $V = abc$	VOLUME $V = \pi r^2 h$
CONE	**SPHERE**	**HEMISPHERE**
SURFACE AREA	**SURFACE AREA**	**SURFACE AREA**
TOTAL $A = \pi r^2 + \pi r l$	$A = 4\pi r^2$	TOTAL $A = 3\pi r^2$
CURVED $A = \pi r l$	VOLUME	CURVED $A = 2\pi r^2$
VOLUME $V = \dfrac{1}{3}\pi r^2 h$	$V = \dfrac{4}{3}\pi r^3$	VOLUME $V = \dfrac{2}{3}\pi r^3$

Example 1:

Find the area of a triangle with a base of 18 inches and a height of 16 inches.

Solution:

Apply the formula of the area of a triangle.

$$Area = \frac{b \times h}{2}$$

Replace the given values in the formula.

$$Area = \frac{18\ in \times 16\ in}{2} = \frac{288\ in^2}{2} = \mathbf{144\ in^2}$$

Example 2:

Find the surface area and volume of the following three-dimensional shape:

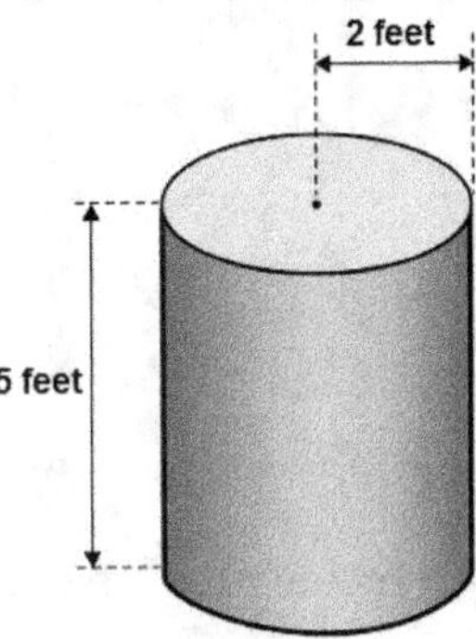

Solution:

Notice that the shape is a cylinder with the following dimensions: radius = 2 ft. and height = 5 ft. Apply the formula for the surface area of a cylinder:

$$A = 2\pi r(r + h)$$

$$A = 2 \cdot 3.14 \cdot 2ft\,(2\,ft + 5\,ft)$$

$$A = (12.56\,ft)(7\,ft) = \mathbf{87.92\,ft^2}$$

Apply the formula for the volume of a cylinder:

$$V = \pi r^2 h$$

$$V = 3.14(2ft)^2(5\,ft) = \mathbf{62.80\,ft^3}$$

Example 3:

The area of a square is 121 square feet. What is the length of the side of the square?

Apply the formula for the area of a square.

$$A = l^2$$

Given A = 121 ft², replace this value in the formula:

$$l^2 = 121\,ft^2$$

Take the square root of both sides:

$$\sqrt{l^2} = \sqrt{121\,ft^2}$$

$$l = 11\,ft$$

Thus, the length of the side of the square is **11 feet**.

1. What is the area of a circle with a radius of 20 inches? (Use $\pi = 3.14$)

    A. 125.6 in^2

    B. 628 in^2

    C. 1,356 in^2

    D. 1,256 in^2

The dimensions of a rectangular box are 6 in. x 15 in. x 8 in.

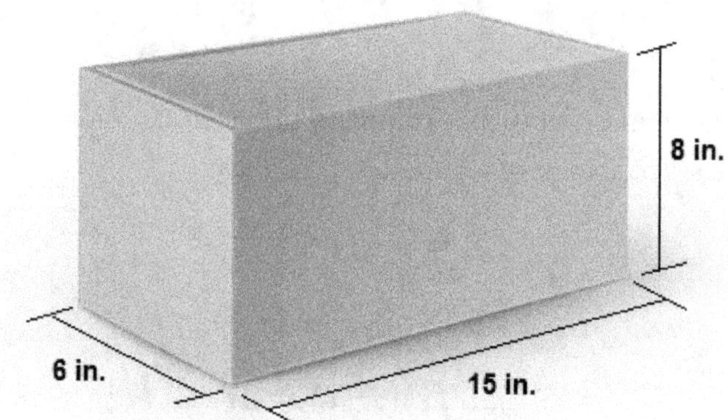

2. What is the total surface area of the box?

    A. 420 in^2

    B. 516 in^2

    C. 480 in^2

    D. 520 in^2

3. What is the volume of the box?

    A. 360 in^3

    B. 800 in^3

    C. 720 in^3

    D. 740 in^3

4. What is the perimeter of the bottom of the box?

    A. 42 in.

    B. 21 in.

C. 28 in.

D. 14 in.

5. What is the circumference of a circle with a radius of 5 feet? (Use $\pi = 3.14$)

   A. 78.5 ft.

   B. 39.25 ft.

   C. 41.35 ft.

   D. 31.4 ft.

6. The perimeter of a square is 48 feet. What is the area of the square?

   A. 576 ft^2

   B. 144 ft^2

   C. 72 ft^2

   D. 192 ft^2

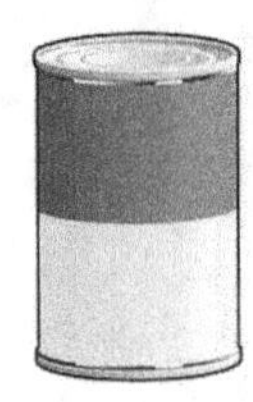

A soup can has a radius of 3 inches and a height of 5 inches.

7. What is the surface area of the can? (Use $\pi = 3.14$)

   A. 150.72 in^2

   B. 94.20 in^2

   C. 112.56 in^2

   D. 142.50 in^2

8. What is the volume of the can? (Use $\pi = 3.14$)

   A. 150.88 in^3

   B. 141.30 in^3

   C. 134.55 in^3

   D. 145.35 in^3

9. What is the base of a triangle whose height is 40 inches and the area is 700 square inches?

   A. 30 inches

   B. 50 inches

   C. 24 inches

   D. 35 inches

10. If the surface area of a sphere is 1, 256 square inches, what is the radius of the sphere? (Use $\pi =$ 3.14)

   A. 10 in.

   B. 20 in

   C. 12 in.

   D. 5 in.

Answer Key:

1) D

2) B

3) C

4) A

5) D

6) B

7) A

8) B

9) D

10) A

Lesson 2: Solve problems with measurement and scale drawings.

Scale drawings show real objects or figures with their sizes accurately reduced or enlarged by a specified ratio called **the scale**. These figures are called **similar figures.**

In two similar figures, the ratio of the lengths of their corresponding sides is called the **scale factor**. To find the scale factor, locate two corresponding sides, one on each figure. Then, write the ratio of the length of one side to the length of the corresponding side in the other figure.

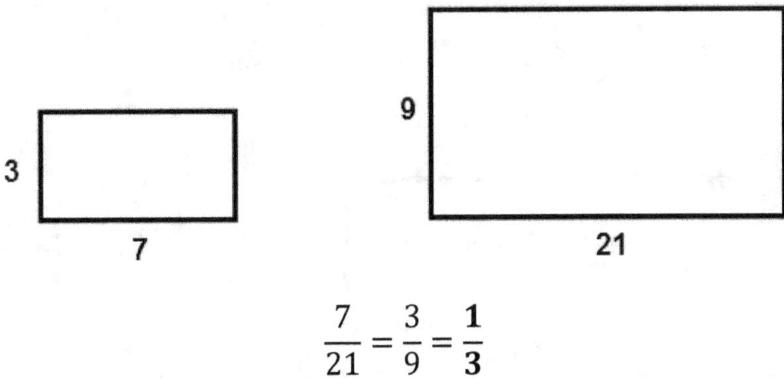

$$\frac{7}{21} = \frac{3}{9} = \frac{1}{3}$$

These two similar rectangles have a scale factor of **1:3** from the small rectangle to the large rectangle. We can interpret and use proportions to solve problems involving dimensions or scale.

Example 1:

A miniature model of a building is made using the scale 2 inches = 8 feet. If the height of the building is 50 feet, what is the height of the miniature model?

Solution:

Let x be the height of the miniature model. Write the proportion that represents the problem.

$$\frac{2 \; inches}{8 \; feet} = \frac{x}{50 \; feet}$$

We have an equation. Now, we solve for x by cross-multiplying.

$$\frac{2 \; inches}{8 \; feet} = \frac{x}{50 \; feet}$$

$$(8 \text{ feet}) \cdot x = (2 \text{ inches}) \cdot (50 \text{ feet})$$

$$\Rightarrow \quad x = \frac{(2 \text{ inches}) \cdot (50 \text{ feet})}{8 \text{ feet}} = \frac{100 \text{ inches} \cdot \text{feet}}{8 \text{ feet}} = 12.50 \text{ inches}$$

Then, the height of the miniature model is **12.50 inches.**

Practice Exercises

1. A map has a scale of 2 inches: 18 miles. If two cities are 9 inches apart on the map, how far are they actually apart?

   A. 81 miles

   B. 162 miles

   C. 72 miles

   D. 96 miles

The following rectangles are similar.

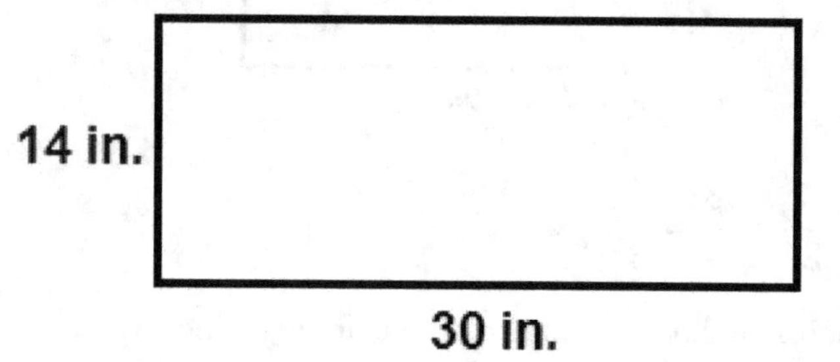

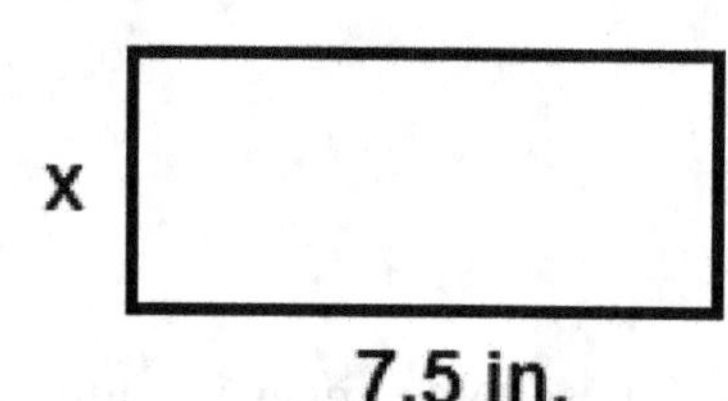

2. What is x?

   A. 4 in.

   B. 4.5 in.

   C. 5 in.

   D. 3.5 in.

3. What is the perimeter of the smaller rectangle?

   A. 11 in.

   B. 17 in.

   C. 22 in.

   D. 23 in.

4. What is the area of the smaller rectangle?

   A. 21.50 in^2

   B. 26.25 in^2

C. 42.45 in^2

D. 25.50 in^2

5. If the scale factor is less than 1, then the size of the new shape is

A. Enlarged.

B. Reduced.

C. Same.

D. None of the above.

6. If the distance on a map represents 3 cm = 18 meters, what is the scale factor?

A. 6: 1

B. 3: 9

C. 1: 9

D. 1: 6

7. Andrew has a scale drawing of his living room. The scale he used was 1:25. In his drawing, his bedroom is 12 inches long and 9.6 inches wide. What are the actual dimensions of his bedroom in feet? (Hint: 1 ft. = 12 in.)

A. Long = 20 ft., wide = 25 ft.

B. Long = 24 ft., wide = 32 ft.

C. Long = 25 ft., wide = 20 ft.

D. Long = 30 ft., wide = 24 ft.

8. If the scale factor is 10/9, then the size of the new shape is

A. Reduced.

B. Enlarged.

C. Same.

D. None of the above.

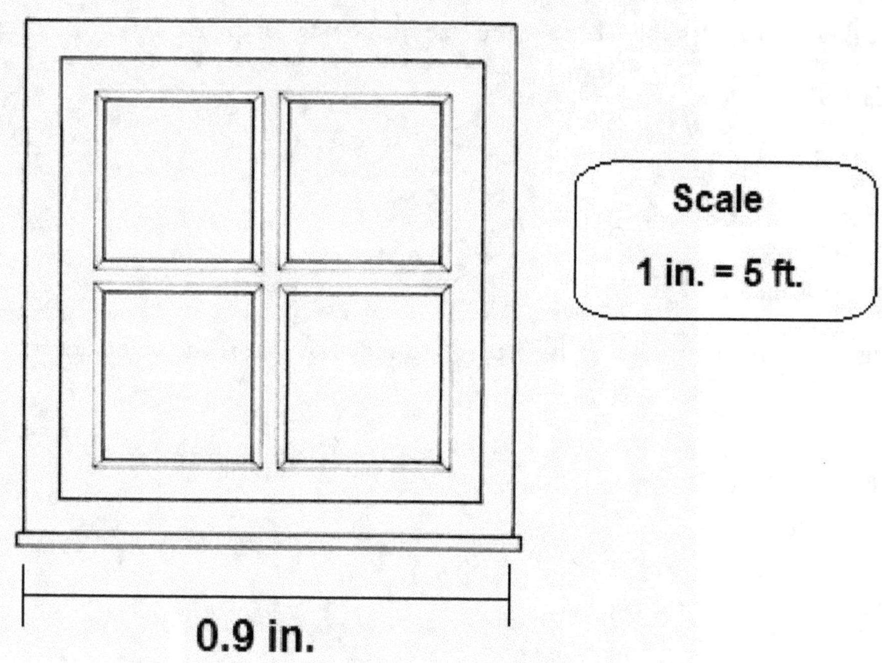

9. What is the perimeter of the actual square window shown in the scale drawing?

   A. 18 in.

   B. 9 ft.

   C. 3.6 in.

   D. 18 ft.

10. What is the area of the actual square window shown in the scale drawing?

   A. 20.25 ft^2

   B. 12.96 in^2

   C. 18 ft^2

   D. 20.55 in^2

1) A

2) D

3) C

4) B

5) B

6) D

7) C

8) B

9) D

10) A

Lesson 3: Understand the Pythagorean Theorem and the concepts of congruence and similarity.

The **Pythagorean Theorem** relates to the sides of a right triangle. In a right triangle, there are two sides called **the legs** that meet at a 90° angle. The side opposite the right angle is known as **the hypotenuse.**

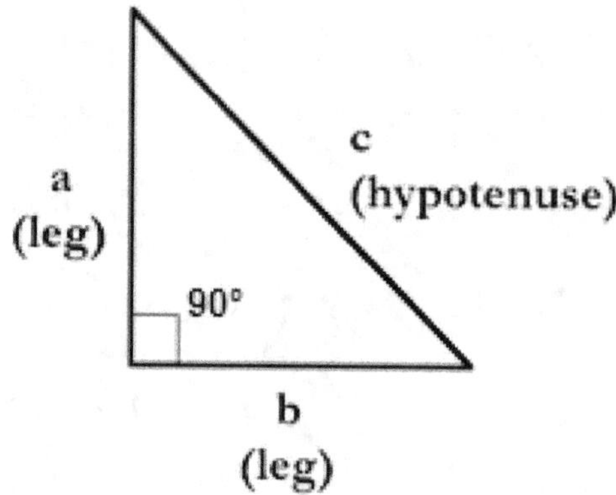

The Pythagorean Theorem says the following:

In a right triangle, the square of the hypotenuse is equal to the sum of the squares of the two legs.

This theorem can be written in one equation:

$$a^2 + b^2 = c^2$$

Congruent Figures

If one shape or geometric figure can be transformed into another using rotations, translations, or reflections, then the figures are congruent. In other words, congruent figures have the same shape and size.

Congruent Figures

Similar Figures

Similar figures have the same shape as the real object but are not the same size. The corresponding angles of similar shapes are equal, and the corresponding sides are proportional. The **scale factor** is the ratio of corresponding side lengths of similar figures.

Example 1:

The following triangle is a right triangle. Find *m*.

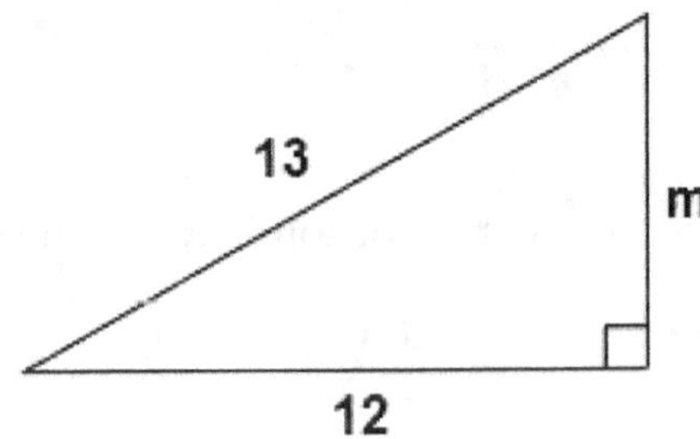

Solution:

Step 1: Notice that *m* is one of the legs of the right triangle. Apply the Pythagorean Theorem.

$$a^2 + b^2 = c^2$$

Here, *m* is one leg (*a*), 12 is the other leg (*b*), and 13 is the hypotenuse (*c*).

$$m^2 + (12)^2 = (13)^2$$

$$m^2 + 144 = 169$$

Step 2: Solve the equation.

$$m^2 + 144 = 169$$

$$m^2 = 169 - 144$$

$$m^2 = 25$$

Step 3: Take the square root of both sides of the equation to eliminate the exponent on the left side.

$$m^2 = 25$$

$$\sqrt{m^2} = \sqrt{25}$$

$$\mathbf{m = 5}$$

Example 2:

The following triangles are similar. What is x?

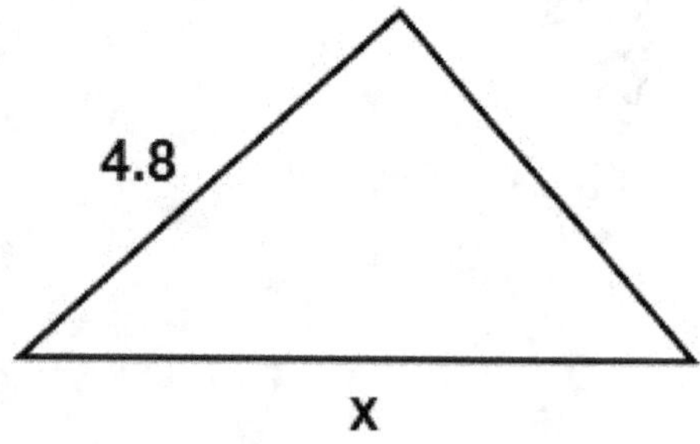

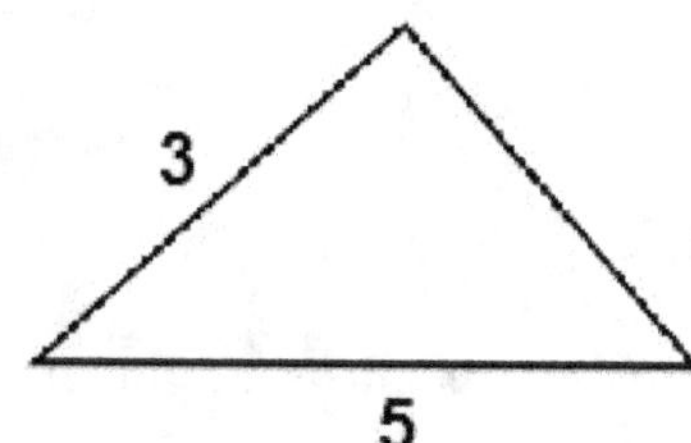

Solution:

Since the triangles are similar, we set up the proportion between the corresponding side lengths.

$$\frac{4.8}{3} = \frac{x}{5}$$

Cross-multiply to solve the equation.

$$\frac{4.8}{3} = \frac{x}{5}$$

$$\Rightarrow 3x = (4.8) \cdot (5)$$

$$3x = 24$$

$$x = \frac{24}{3} = \mathbf{8}$$

Practice Exercises

The following right triangles are similar.

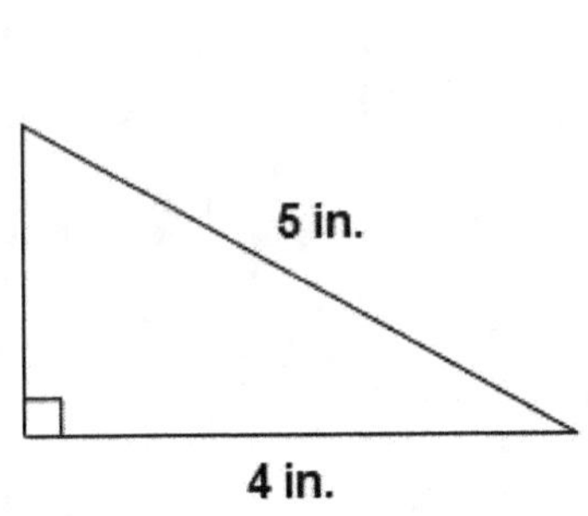

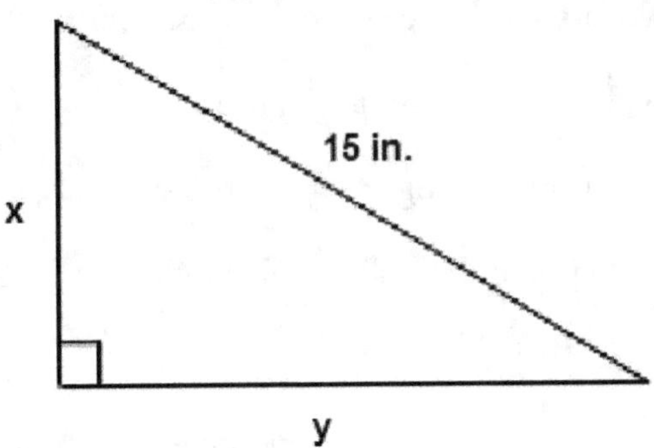

1. What is y?

   A. 10 in.

   B. 12 in.

   C. 9 in.

   D. 8 in.

2. What is x?

   A. 8 in.

   B. 10 in.

   C. 7 in.

   D. 9 in.

3. What is the perimeter of the larger triangle?

   A. 36 in.

   B. 32 in.

   C. 28 in.

   D. 12 in.

4. What is the area of the smaller triangle?

   A. 12 in^2

   B. 8 in^2

C. 6 in^2

D. 10 in^2

5. Which of the following is true?

   A. Two similar figures have the same perimeter.

   B. Rotations create similar figures.

   C. Two congruent figures have the same area.

   D. The hypotenuse is the smaller side of a right triangle.

The rectangles A and B are congruent.

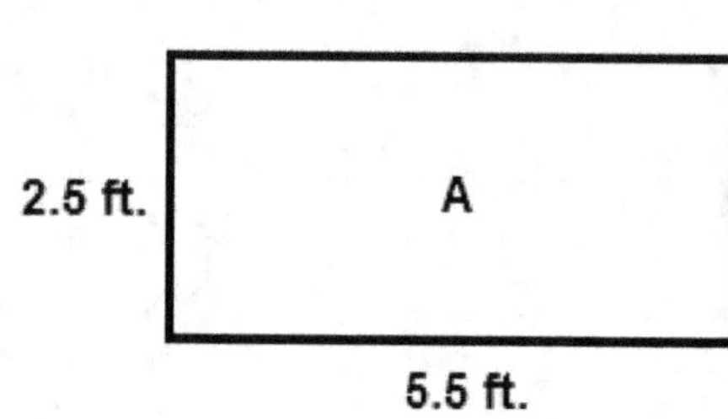

6. What is the perimeter of Rectangle B?

   A. 8 ft.

   B. 16 ft.

   C. 20 ft.

   D. 15 ft.

7. What is the area of Rectangle B?

   A. 13.75 ft^2

   B. 8 ft^2

   C. 15.50 ft^2

   D. 12 ft^2

8. Two legs of a right triangle measure 2 inches and 5 inches. What is the length of the hypotenuse?

   A. $\sqrt{14}$ in.

   B. 29 in.

   C. $\sqrt{29}$ in.

   D. 7 in.

9. A rectangular field is 30 yards long, and the length of one diagonal of the field is 34 yards. What is the width of the field?

   A. 16 yards

   B. 19 yards

   C. 15 yards

   D. 21 yards

10. Two circles, Circle A and Circle B, are congruent to each other. If the radius of Circle A is 9 inches, what is the circumference of Circle B?

   A. 9π in.

   B. 18π in.

   C. 81π in.

   D. 4.5π in.

Answer Key:

1) B	6) B
2) D	7) A
3) A	8) C
4) C	9) A
5) C	10) B

Answer the following reflection questions and feel free to discuss your responses with your teacher or a classmate.

1- What math ideas and principles did you learn in this chapter?

2- What new math concepts did you learn?

3- What procedures or methods did you practice in this chapter?

4- What aspect of this chapter is still not 100% clear to you?

5- What else do you want your teacher to know?

CHAPTER 5:
DATA ANALYSIS, STATISTICS, AND PROBABILITY

Lesson 1: Understand statistical variability concepts and recognize deviations from patterns.

One important aspect of the distribution of data is where its center is located. The **mean, median, and mode** are measures of the center of a set of data. They are called **measures of central tendency**. They provide a summary measure to describe a data set with a single value that represents the middle or center of the distribution.

- The mean (or average) is the sum of all the values in the set divided by the number of values in the set.

- The **median** is the middle value in a sorted list of numbers.

- The **mode** is the most common number that appears in a set of data.

The **deviations** from the pattern occur when certain data points do not fit the overall pattern. For example, a data set can be generally symmetrical except for one value that does not fit the pattern.

Here are two specific types of deviations:

Outliers: These are data points that are far from other data points. The mean is the only measure of central tendency that is always affected by an outlier.

Gaps: Some data sets may have gaps where no data points exist.

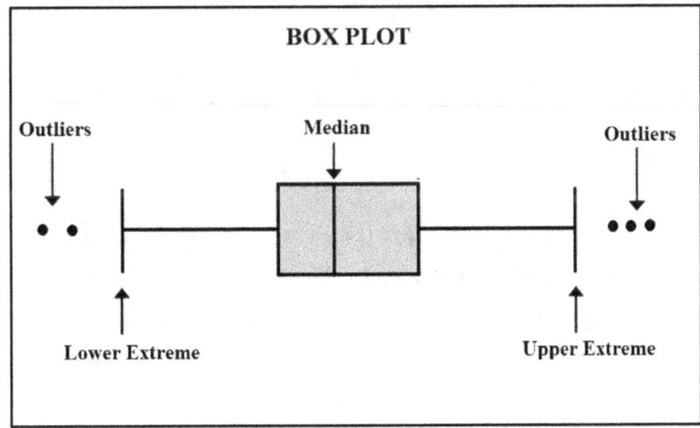

The mean has one main disadvantage: it is particularly susceptible to the influence of outliers. In other words, the mean is the only measure of central tendency that is always affected by an outlier.

In **a symmetrical distribution of data**, the mean is the same number as the median and mode.

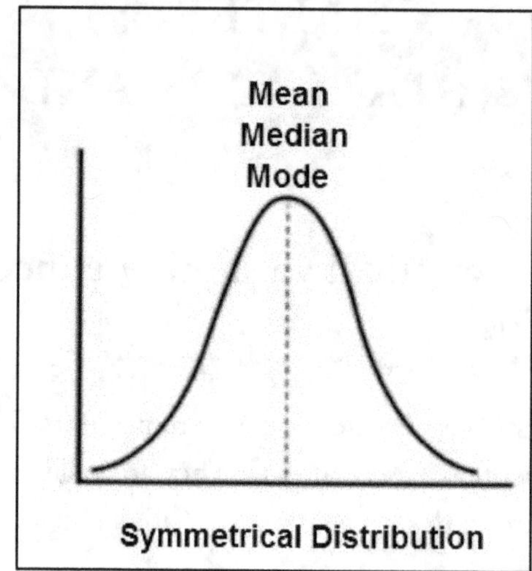

Measures of spread describe how similar or varied the set of observed values is. The simplest way to find the spread in a data set is to identify **the range**, which is the difference between the highest and lowest values. A larger range indicates a greater spread in the data.

Example 1:

Find the mean, median, mode, and range of the following set of data: 50, 20, 60, 80, 60, 90, 30, 60, 75, and 65.

Solution:

To calculate the mean, add all the numbers in the set together. After, divide the sum by the number of values in the set. (There are 10 numbers.)

$$\text{Mean} = \frac{50 + 20 + 60 + 80 + 60 + 90 + 30 + 60 + 75 + 65}{10} = \frac{590}{10} = 59$$

Then, the mean is **59**.

To calculate the median, first place all the values in numerical order.

20, 30, 50, 60, 60, 60, 65, 75, 80, 90

If we have an odd number of values, the median is the middle number. However, if we have an even number of values, the median will be the mean of the two values in the center of the data set. We have an even number of values, so we must calculate the mean of the two central values:

20, 30, 50, 60, **60, 60**, 65, 75, 80, 90

$$\text{Mean} = \frac{60 + 60}{2} = \frac{120}{2} = 60$$

Then, the median is **60.**

The mode is the value that occurs most often. Notice that the value of 60 appears three times. Thus, the mode is **60.**

To calculate the range of the data set, subtract the lowest value from the highest value.

Range = $90 - 20 =$ **70**

Practice Exercises

> Kirby bowled 8 games last month. His scores are 162, 155, 72, 138, 145, 138, 190, and 160.

1. What is the mean of Kirby's scores?

    A. 160

    B. 190

    C. 140

    D. 145

2. What is the median of Kirby's scores?

    A. 150

    B. 145

    C. 144

    D. 155

3. What is the mode of Kirby's scores?

    A. 145

    B. 72

    C. 138

    D. There is no mode.

4. What is the range of Kirby's scores?

   A. 115

   B. 118

   C. 190

   D. 135

5. What is the outlier in the data set, if one exists?

   A. 138

   B. 190

   C. 72

   D. There is no outlier.

6. Which of the following is the measure for the center of a distribution of data?

   A. Outlier

   B. Range

   C. Symmetrical distribution

   D. Median

> A group of diners was asked how much they would pay for a meal. Their responses were as follows: $9.80, $8.50, $9, $13, $10, $12, $11, $20, $15 and x.

7. If the mean of the data set is $12.23, what is x?

   A. $14

   B. $15.25

   C. $16

   D. $14.75

8. What is the median of the data set?

   A. $12.50

   B. $13.00

C. $11.50

D. $11.25

9. What is the mode of the data set?

A. $9.80

B. $11

C. $14

D. There is no mode.

10. What is the range of the data set?

A. $11.50

B. $12

C. $13.75

D. $13

Answer Key:

1) D

2) A

3) C

4) B

5) C

6) D

7) A

8) C

9) D

10) A

Lesson 2: Understand and apply the concept of probability.

The probability of a specified event is the chance or likelihood that it will occur. It is determined by dividing the favorable outcomes by the total number of outcomes. Thus, probability is **always a number between 0 and 1.**

We can see the mean of probability in the following scale.

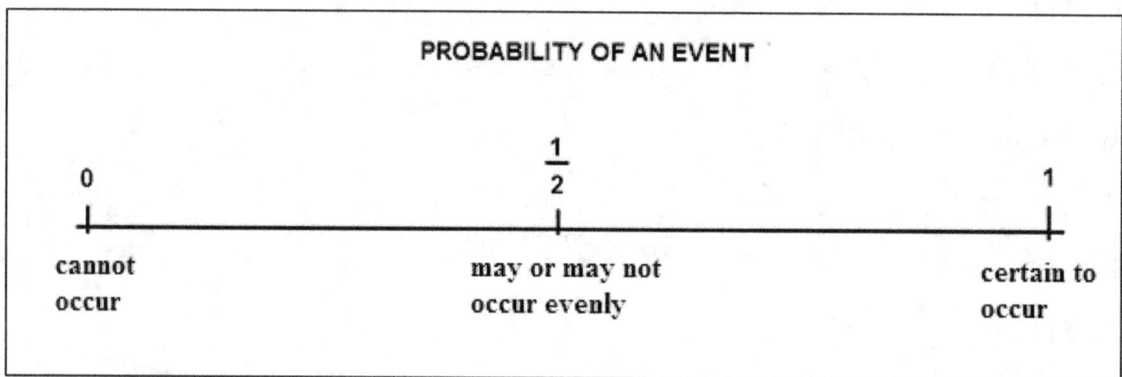

In other words, an event with a **0** probability can never happen because the favorable outcome is zero. If an event has a **1** probability, it will certainly happen because there are the same number of favorable outcomes as total outcomes.

If an event has a ½ probability, it has an equal chance of happening or not happening. If an event has a probability between **0** and **0.5**, then it is unlikely to happen but not impossible. If an event has a probability between **0.5** and **1**, then it is likely to happen but not certain.

Probabilities can be expressed in terms of ratios. Since any ratio can be turned into a fraction, decimal, or percent, we can also turn any probability into a **fraction, decimal, or percent.** For example, the **probability that a fair coin lands on the tail is ½. This probability can be expressed in several forms:**

$$P = \frac{1}{2}, \qquad P = 0.5, \qquad P = 50\%$$

Example 1:

Leslie has a bag with 26 cherries, 16 sweet and 10 sour. If she picks a cherry at random, what is the probability that it will be sweet?

Solution:

There are 26 possible cherries that could be picked, so the number of possible outcomes is 26. Of these 26 possible outcomes, 16 are favorable (sweet).

Here is the probability that the cherry will be sweet:

$$Probability = \frac{Number\ of\ ways\ it\ can\ happen}{Total\ number\ of\ outcomes} = \frac{16}{26} = \frac{8}{13}$$

Practice Exercises

1. Which of the following events has a probability that equals 1?

   A. A head will come up in a coin toss.

   B. Pick a card from a 52 deck of cards and get an ace.

   C. Choose a blue ball from a bag that has only blue balls.

   D. Sleep 10 hours.

2. A number from 1 to 20 is chosen at random. What is the probability of choosing an odd number?

   A. 50%

   B. 25%

   C. 75%

   D. 100%

A test was given to a group of students whose grades and gender are summarized below:

	Grade A	Grade B	Grade C	Total
Male	10	15	14	39
Female	8	20	8	36
Total	18	35	22	75

3. If one student was chosen randomly, what is the probability that the student was female?

   A. 0.27

   B. 0.11

   C. 0.35

   D. 0.48

4. If one student was chosen randomly, what is the probability that the student was male?

   A. 0.48

   B. 0.52

   C. 0.20

   D. 0.25

5. If one student was chosen randomly, what is the probability that the student would get A?

   A. 0.24

   B. 0.45

   C. 0.16

   D. 0.1

6. What is the probability of rolling 7 with a six-sided die?

   A. 1/6

   B. 1/7

   C. 1

   D. 0

7. What is the probability of tossing a six-sided die and getting a number less than 3?

   A. 1/3

   B. 1/2

   C. 1/6

   D. 1/4

8. Which of the following cannot be a probability?

   A. 0.9%

   B. 0.918

   C. 12/11

   D. 1/200

9. Warren writes each letter of the alphabet on a different slip of paper and puts the slips into a hat. What is the probability of drawing one slip of paper from the hat randomly and getting a consonant?

   A. 22/26

   B. 21/26

   C. 5/13

   D. 2/13

10. A ball is drawn randomly from a jar that contains 18 black balls, 12 white balls, and 10 green balls. What is the probability of getting a white ball?

   A. 0.30

   B. 0.15

   C. 0.42

   D. 0.36

Answer Key:

1) C

2) A

3) D

4) B

5) A

6) D

7) A

8) C

9) B

10) A

Answer the following reflection questions and feel free to discuss your responses with your teacher or a classmate.

1- What math ideas and principles did you learn in this chapter?

2- What new math concepts did you learn?

3- What procedures or methods did you practice in this chapter?

4- What aspect of this chapter is still not 100% clear to you?

5- What else do you want your teacher to know?

CHAPTER 6:
PURE MATHEMATICS

Practice Exercises

1. Kirk fills his gas tank with 15 gallons of premium gas for \$59.25. How much would it cost to fill a 60-gallon tank?

2. Rose worked 10 months out of the year. What percent of the year did she work?

3. Simplify the following expression:

$$\frac{7^7 \cdot 7}{7^0}$$

4. Frank has a job that pays him \$25.50 per hour. Assume a working week has 40 hours, and there are 52 weeks in the year. Calculate Frank's annual salary.

5. Solve the following equation:

$$100 = 15 + 5m$$

6. Write a linear inequality for the following situation. (Use x for the unknown value)

I have no more than \$1, 245.67 in my savings account.

7. Find the perimeter of the following figure:

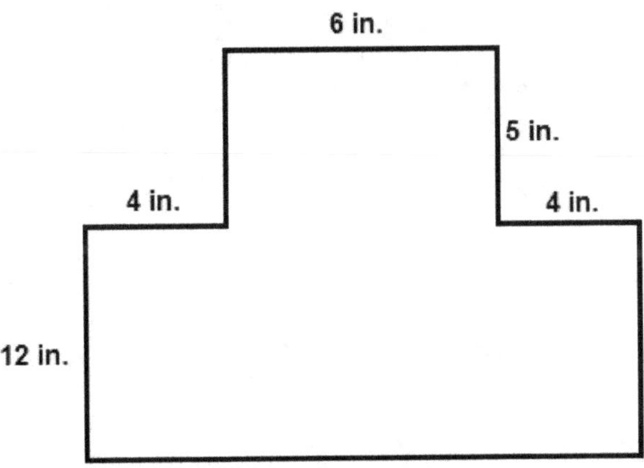

8. The surface area of a cube is 486 square feet. What is the volume of the cube?

9. What is the probability that a month picked at random starts with the letter A? (Express your answer as a fraction.)

10. The following data set shows a town's daily high temperature, in degrees Celsius, for 7 days.

$$35.5, 37.2, 35.8, 39.2, 34.8, 36.6, 34.8$$

Find the median of the data set.

Answer Key:

1) $237

2) 83.3%

3) 7^8

4) $53, 040

5) $m = 17$

6) $x \leq 1, 245.67$

7) 62 in.

8) 729 cubic feet

9) 1/6

10) 35.8

REFLECTION ON LEARNING

Answer the following reflection questions and discuss your responses with your teacher or a classmate.

1- How do you feel about your performance on the exercise?

2- What types of questions were difficult for you?

3- How do you feel about your time management strategies?

4- What specific things do you want to do differently next time? List them.

5- What math functions or content areas do you want to review? List them.

6- What else do you want your teacher to know?

1. Rachel bought eight gallons of paint. She fills the paint equally into ten bottles. A quarter of a gallon of paint is left. What is the volume of paint in one bottle?

   A. 1.025 gallons

   B. 0.80 gallons

   C. 0.775 gallons

   D. 0.825 gallons

2. Calculate $\frac{1}{2}\left(\frac{3}{5} + \frac{2}{3}\right)$

   A. 19/15

   B. 1/30

   C. 3/10

   D. 19/30

3. Billy drives 84 miles in 8/5 hours. Find the unit rate in miles per hour.

   A. 52.50 miles per hour

   B. 55 miles per hour

   C. 134.40 miles per hour

   D. 62.50 miles per hour

4. 5.5% of the cost of an item was tax. If the tax was $12.98, what was the cost of the item?

   A. $245

   B. $236

   C. $280

   D. $118

5. Sarah can write six essays in one week. Assuming she works at this constant rate, how many essays can she write in 21 days?

   A. 18

   B. 36

   C. 126

D. 45

6. Which of the following is equivalent to $10^{10} \cdot 100$?

    A. 1000^{10}

    B. 10^{1000}

    C. 10^8

    D. 10^{12}

7. What is k?

$$\frac{(3^3)^3}{3^6} = 3^k$$

    A. 6

    B. 3

    C. 2

    D. 0

Look at the following receipt:

```
WALL-MART-SUPERSTORE
(888) 888 - 8888
MANAGER TOD LINGA
888 WALL STORE ST
WALL ST CITY, LA 88888
ST# 2323 OP#     23432435 TE#     51        TR#  4354
HAND TOWEL       075953630184                2.97 X
GATORADE         068949055223                2.00 X
T-SHIRT          036231552452               16.88 X
PUSH PINS        088348997350                1.24 X
                          SUBTOTAL          23.09
          TAX 1           7.89%              2.90
          TAX 2           4.90%              1.28
                            TOTAL               ?
                    CREDIT  TEND
                    CHANGE DUE               0.00
ACCOUNT #              **** **** ***9999
APPROVAL # 77W166
REF # 307171075528
TERMINAL # 5419885359
```

8. How many items were purchased?

    A. 5

    B. 4

    C. 6

    D. 3

9. What is the subtotal amount?

    A. $16.88

    B. $2.90

    C. $23.09

    D. $27.50

10. What is the total amount?

    A. $28.12

    B. $23.09

    C. $26.99

    D. $27.27

11. Which item is the cheapest?

    A. Hand towel

    B. Push pins

    C. T-shirt

    D. Gatorade

12. What is the cost of nine hand towels?

    A. $26.73

    B. $25.86

    C. $27.00

    D. $25.99

The perimeter of the following rectangle is 54 inches.

12 in.

2x + 3

13. What is x?

   A. 5

   B. 7

   C. 9

   D. 6

14. What is the area of the rectangle?

   A. 192 in^2

   B. 245 in^2

   C. 180 in^2

   D. 144 in^2

15. If the width of the rectangle is equal to the length, what is x?

   A. 4.5

   B. 6

   C. 5.5

   D. 3

16. Solve the following inequality:

$$24 - 2x \leq 52$$

   A. $x \geq -14$

   B. $x \leq -14$

   C. $x \leq 14$

   D. $x \geq 14$

17. A farmer cuts a 156-foot fence into two pieces of different sizes. The longer piece is three times as long as the shorter piece. How long is the longer piece?

A. 115 ft.

B. 117 ft.

C. 72 ft.

D. 120 ft.

18. The cost to repair a Smart TV is \$270 plus \$18 per hour for labor. What is the independent variable in this situation?

A. The total cost to repair

B. \$18 per hour

C. The number of hours for labor

D. The price of the Smart TV

19. Which of the following represents a linear equation?

A. $h = 0.4t^2$

B. $y = x + 1$

C. $y = 3/x$

D. $x = y^3$

20. Which equation represents a proportional relationship?

A. $y = 3x - 5$

B. $x = 3y + 9$

C. $y = 4$

D. $y = 0.5x$

21. Which of the following graphs represents a proportional relationship?

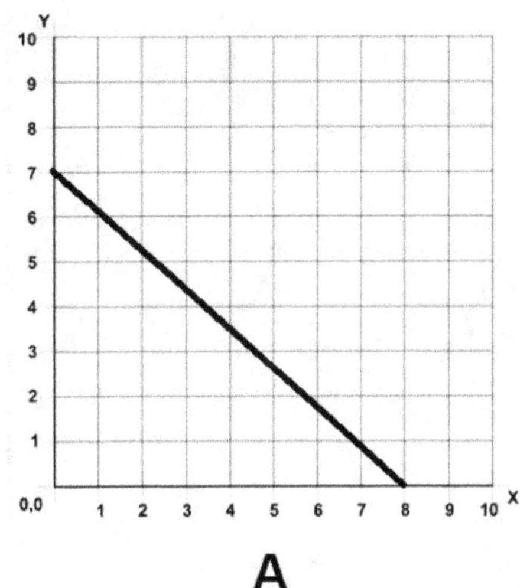

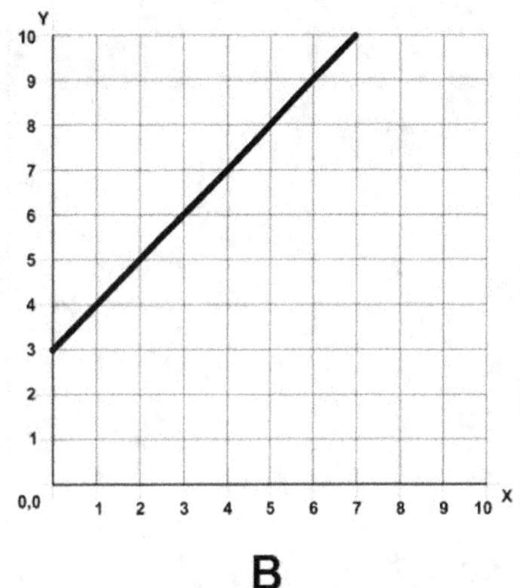

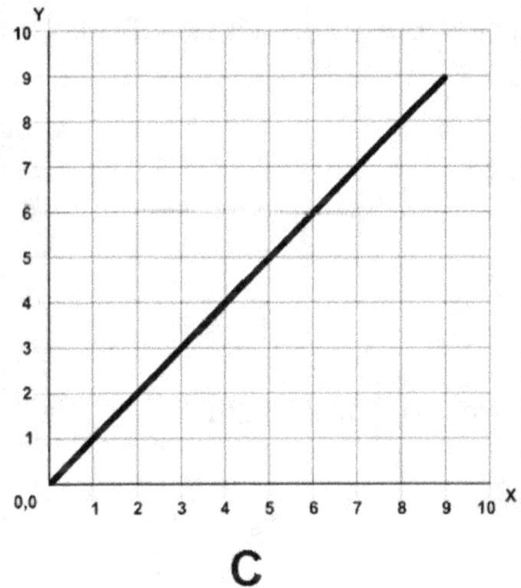

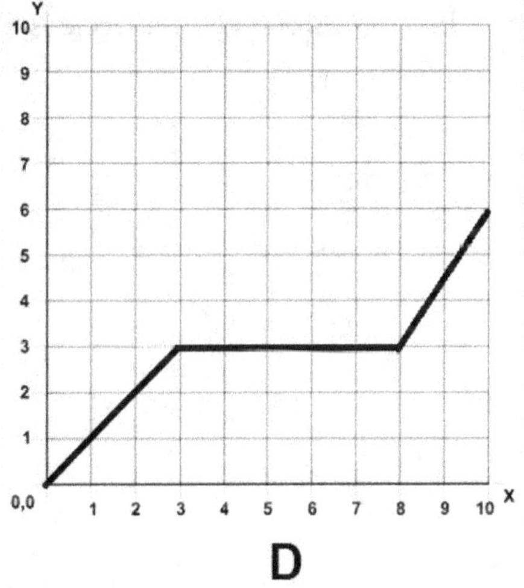

A. Graph C

B. Graph D

C. Graph A

D. Graph B

22. What is the area of the following shape?

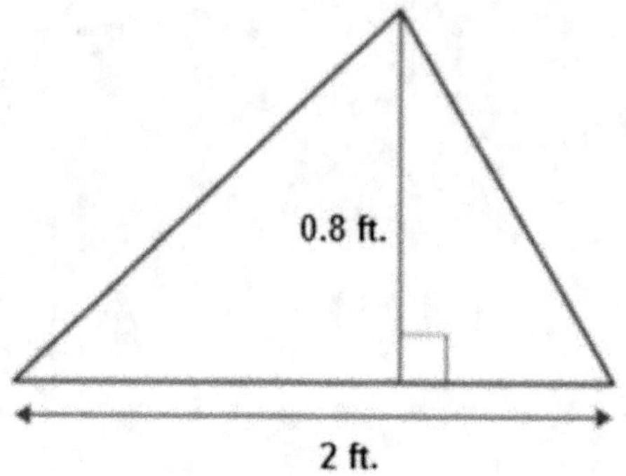

A. 1.6 ft²

B. 0.8 ft²

C. 1.8 ft²

D. 0.9 ft²

23. The circumference of a circle is 56.52 inches. What is the area of the circle? (Use $\pi = 3.14$)

A. 254.34 in²

B. 56.52 in²

C. 127.17 in²

D. 175.84 in²

The triangle ABC, an isosceles triangle, has two sides of equal length.

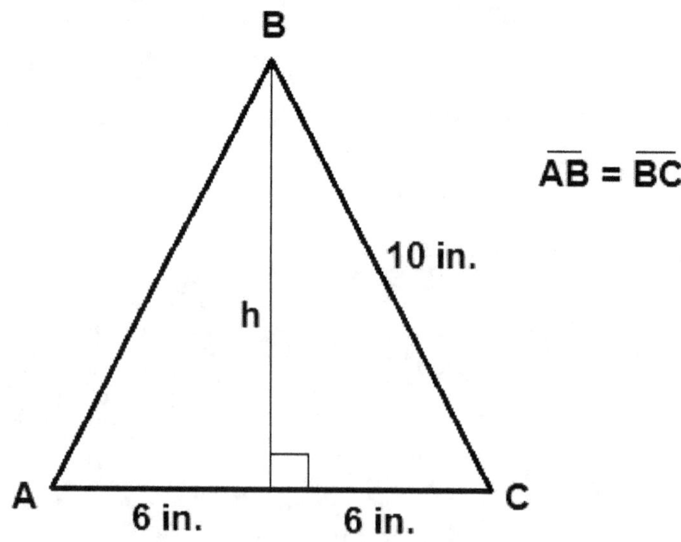

24. What is the height of the triangle ABC?

   A. 7 in.

   B. 5 in.

   C. 8 in.

   D. 6 in.

25. What is the area of the triangle ABC?

   A. 18 in^2

   B. 24 in^2

   C. 32 in^2

   D. 48 in^2

26. What is the perimeter of the triangle ABC?

   A. 26 in.

   B. 32 in.

   C. 16 in.

   D. 24 in.

27. The dimensions of a rectangular box are 10 in. x 12 in. x k in. The volume of the box is 1,800 cubic inches. What is k?

   A. 12 in.

   B. 18 in.

   C. 15 in.

   D. 16 in.

28. A plan of a house uses the scale 1 in. = 6.5 ft. What is the distance on the plan for the actual distance of 55.9 feet?

   A. 8.6 in.

   B. 12.5 in.

   C. 62.4 in.

   D. 363.35 in.

The heights of a group of footballers in meters
are listed below:
1.85, 1.91, 1.75, 1.83, 1.85, 1.90, 1.92, and 1.88

29. What is the mean of the data set?

    A. 1.86

    B. 1.85

    C. 1.90

    D. 1.88

30. What is the median of the data set?

    A. 1.860

    B. 1.870

    C. 1.865

    D. 1.868

31. What is the mode of the data set?

    A. 1.90

    B. 1.85

    C. 1.75

    D. There is no mode.

32. What is the range of the data set?

    A. 0.17

    B. 0.19

    C. 1.10

    D. 0.22

A spinner has 8 equal sectors colored as shown below.

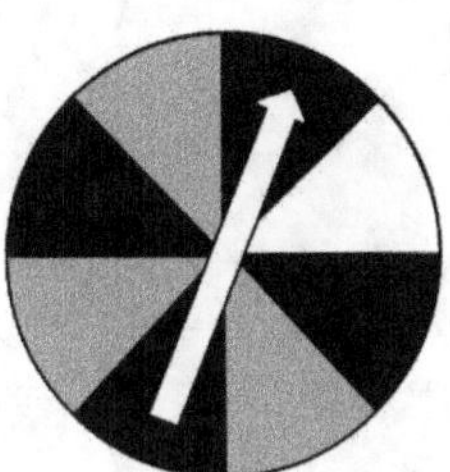

33. What is the probability of landing on black after spinning the spinner?

    A. 0.80

    B. 0.60

    C. 0.25

    D. 0.50

34. What is the probability of landing on white after spinning the spinner?

    A. 0.125

    B. 0.250

    C. 0.555

    D. 0.333

35. What is the probability of landing on green after spinning the spinner?

    A. 0.10

    B. 0.01

    C. 0.25

    D. 0

36. If it is Saturday, what is the probability that tomorrow is Sunday?

    A. 50%

    B. 75%

    C. 90%

    D. 100%

1. C	13. D	25. D
2. D	14. C	26. B
3. A	15. A	27. C
4. B	16. A	28. A
5. A	17. B	29. A
6. D	18. C	30. C
7. B	19. B	31. B
8. B	20. D	32. A
9. C	21. A	33. D
10. D	22. B	34. A
11. B	23. A	35. D
12. 1A	24. C	36. D

Answer the following reflection questions and discuss your responses with your teacher or a classmate.

1- How do you feel about your performance on the test?

2- What types of questions were difficult for you?

3- How do you feel about your time management strategies?

4- What specific things do you want to do differently next time? List them.

5- What math functions or content areas do you want to review? List them.

6- What else do you want your teacher to know?

About CBL

At CBL, we promote systematic solutions, learner-centered textbooks, and forward-thinking strategies in adult education, workforce development, and vocational training. Our diverse solutions and products are intricately designed to enrich students' learning experiences while making the job of busy, hard-working adult instructors easier.

CBL takes pride in publishing student-centered textbooks designed to prepare learners for CASAS, TABE 11&12, HiSET, and GED assessments and assists instructors in covering course curricula and standards with confidence.

Our publications also include teaching guides, test prep tools, and study guides that foster reflective learning, ensuring sustained engagement in active learning. Find our meticulously crafted textbooks on our book page (cbledu.com) or major platforms like Amazon, Barnes & Noble, and Ingram Spark.

CBL also guides adult education and workforce programs in establishing robust professional development programs—training, peer-mentoring, coaching, community of practices (CoPs), and instructional systems— fostering a culture of continuous improvement and contributing to higher learner retention and success rates. We also offer workshops and PD sessions for adult educators and classroom instructors.

If you have questions about instructional systems, textbooks, or student learning and retention, contact us today at teamcbl@cbledu.com or 410-960-4082.